Porch Light to the Longshoreman

poems by

Colleen Alles

Finishing Line Press
Georgetown, Kentucky

Porch Light to the Longshoreman

ACKNOWLEDGMENTS

"Reeds Lake" originally appears in the Poetry Society of Michigan's
publication, *Peninsula Poets*, Volume 76-1.

Publisher: Leah Maines
Editor: Christen Kincaid
Cover Art: Matthew Dudzik
Author Photo: Megan Davis, silvergalleryphotography.com
Cover Design: Elizabeth Maines McCleavy

Printed in the USA on acid-free paper.
Order online: www.finishinglinepress.com
also available on amazon.com

Author inquiries and mail orders:
Finishing Line Press
P. O. Box 1626
Georgetown, Kentucky 40324
U. S. A.

Table of Contents

for my family

Possible Scene of an Accident

Forgive me for drinking
all the coffee today.

I didn't start a second pot
before I set out for the morning,
as though at the urging of some great
wilderness explorer
who raised his hat, winked at me, and
with a coal black voice said *go.*

Who knows what will happen today.

Not the farmhouse on the corner,
not the roads glistening still with rain

Who knows what will happen at this intersection
where this street greets the next.

Maybe you can tell me tonight,
when I finally
make my way home
it'll be dark again.
I'll hope to find you wiping your mug
clean from the kitchen sink,
then mine,
then the restlessness
from my eyes left over
from this morning.

Daydream

It was the song on the radio, you say. It was the light
hangover you still feel from last night that lays

not unpleasantly on your mind, turning it over
on this road, letting your thoughts wander

from the curve of my cheek, my lips,
my thigh, and the bends of this road.

You were staring at the birds gathering in roadside
trees and without realizing, you were looking for

my favorite, my songbird. Or you were looking for
any clue that the brightest among them

would suddenly send out a silent call, rally her troops,
begin to take flight without you.

Reeds Lake

A friend of mine was married here, by
this small lake, and that day my feet did nothing
but sink into the sand on the shore when I
was supposed to be pledging my
intention to do all I could to support
their union. The sun was beating down
on my bare shoulders, and I wondered how
many people had married by this lake,
which is small but quite deep. Deep
enough that once someone deliberately
sank a dilapidated boat into the folds
of its waves, rather than take the trouble
to pull it to shore. True story. As I stood there
I also tried to hush the part of my mind that
most likes to lose itself to imagination, because
it was pushing me to remember when I once
read in a book how many people had drowned
in this lake, too. Not many. A handful, and
that happened early, before our modern day
precautions or the tools we developed to measure
the water's depth, communicate about dangers.
Still. The vows were exchanged, then
the kissing, the clapping, the music sneaking
up on us from behind. I tried not to think of
what deep dull waves can do, of what we all
can do to one another treading side by side
year after year. Later, still filled with champagne,
I removed my shoes, much to the delight
of my feet. Many particles of sand fell from my toes
to the carpet and without needing
to look, I knew a lot of those grains would soon
wrestle freely in our bed sheets, gliding past
my ankles, my calves, gradually beating away
next to me onto the shores of your skin.

Outbound Mail

If I had to guess,
the stiff invitation's still wedged under
the eaves, wondering when
I'll see you. If. When. I see you
again without armor and

it's like watching a thousand vowels
and consonants arrange and rearrange,
falling all over themselves, like me,
spilling in all forms of order, trying so hard
to say the right thing. To you.

Keep our distance, on a postcard.
Have all the odd thoughts outlawed.

Sure, but then there's a morning
of laying down all the heavy parts,
of shedding, of being weightless, free:
spinning around downtown streets

and you sure don't look so
convicted in your decision, to me.

Back at the house
it's mystified the mailman again.
That card has disappeared.
It's the third time this week.

Make up your mind lady,
I imagine he says. How hard can it be?
He shakes his head, leaves me with bills.
You want to say it, or you don't.
You'll keep it to yourself,

or you won't.

Instructions for Living in a Small House

When you sneeze in the bathroom, I will bless you from the kitchen.
I hear what you say on the phone. I nod to what you sing in the shower.

Know there are no secrets, and privacy is for outside these walls.

When a cake is baked, the sweetness touches every room.
When it's burned, you won't forget for weeks.

Don't bother that the mail carrier smiles as she walks down the front
sidewalk; she just thinks it's cute is all.

It isn't the house's fault there is no linen closet, no optimal place to put
your muddy boots.

This house isn't being small to make you mad.

Of course it would be nice to have wider hallways. Maybe you don't
always want to press your body against mine when you pass.

Even if you should.

It's nice to call for you and know you'll hear me wherever you are.

Thanks to this house, I know your favorite curse word, and even some
of your prayers.

The most important one:

Every night, a million people wish they were this close. They wish the
walls of their homes would shrink around them, hold them tight, tuck
them into a swaddle at the close of each night,

the way this one always seems to do.

Association of Commerce Building

To know a building you must pace its corners, then tuck yourself
snug in its dark recesses. You can compare its history to your
own. It changes. A picture etches your mind. If someone
were to ask what it is about this building, a misty
representation forms from the impressions and
shapes you salvage in the messy archives of
your heart. To know a building you ought
to pull its pieces into your own interior,
take its imperfect arches as fingerprints
melted on your own. Find its cornerstone
and decide if you'd ever mount a wrecking
ball upon someone else's threat to tear it down.
Delight that it stands as many years as you might.
Step heavily as you leave, as its dirt and dust adhere
to your soles, gently to be left behind everywhere you go.

Auditorium Interior

A crowd has gathered here, and people
are shuffling their expectations.
Don't be afraid to tell them
a long time ago, I decided I love you.
I feel your palm pressed into my hand.
When I see a road wet with rain, in the puddles
there's the perfect almond arc of your eyes.
Every grandmother in our line wants to hold you.

A long time ago, I decided I love you
and now you're the porch light to the longshoreman
weary from a day in the blowing rain.
You have all your expectations of adventure
pressed into the palm of your hand.
You have your grandmother's name.
Open your eyes. They want to hear you.
I love you. Don't be afraid to tell them.

Vigil

Tell the deer here to come
and keep coming.
It's safe and lovely
and she can bring her fawn.
I'll wonder if she knows
what I do now:

so much of having young
is saying yes, I know
this is delightful
but you can't make
this much noise.

Yes, the moon at this hour
as it falls on this grove
of trees is changing
the way I see everything

but you need to go to sleep.
And sleep, and dream.
It's safe and lovely.
I'll sit with you.
I'll keep watch.
I'll hold a vigil
for you
as long
as I can.

Tribute to a Kiss

If you know
why you woke me at 5 a.m.
you're not saying.

Hunger, sure, but you're
more interested in pulling my hair
and grabbing my chin, touching your toes.

You weren't dreaming as I was
of someone you loved
but probably wronged
long ago, when I told myself
I didn't know any better.
I was young.

In 9th grade Biology,
our teacher had us gently prick our lips
with straight pins to demonstrate
why kissing feels so good.
All those nerves lay in wait.

In a way, it was not something
to tell teenagers but bless him,
he did anyway.

Otherwise, this whole business does seem absurd.

People showing affection by putting their mouths
on your skin
gently sucking in.

I kiss your ear and you laugh.

Maybe this is why I'm here
at 5 a.m.

Maybe you had a dream about
how good it feels to be kissed
and just can't wait anymore.

I slide my bottom lip along your hairline and you smile.
I imagine all the nerves and receptors in your skin waking
up, looking at each other.

Yes, they say.
This feeling's amazing.
Kiss me again.
Kiss me again.

Silver Springs

I hate the way my dog looks at me when I put
Silver Springs on repeat and tell him over and over
he'll never get away from the sound of the woman
who loves him.

But he owes me.

Earlier, once the coffee
had pulled the stiffness
from my bones
and I'd slipped into my sneakers,

I imagined the miles I would run in this quiet neighborhood,
setting a personal best at every street. But instead I

was reaching for the frayed red leash, and I took
that damn hound dog,
made my slowest time over and over as we
wandered from tree to tree, his nose
never leaving the ground.

Marriage

First, find a level place on the Earth.

Remove the trees, even though it feels like a shame.

Ensure this is a flat place,
a solid, certain area.

In fact, this might be the most important step.
Don't skip this one.

If you hurry too fast to find the right
well-squared piece of land, the
remaining steps won't matter.

You will want
to take your time
with the cornerstone.

You will need
the heaviest brick
in your corner.

I'm no architect,
but the rest is
all artistry and physics,
a polite and ginger defiance of gravity.

The construction of a building
puffing out its chest with steel trusses
so it won't someday
cave in on itself.

After some time, the roof will follow, and then, other people
may enter.

For now, wonder at the vertical slats, the piles of plywood,
the perfect shadows all this casts on the ground
you chose.

New Stove

It won't be as easy as I am promising.

But will you still consent to carry
my heavy body
over your threshold,
scoot me into a corner,
keep me around

long after I've passed
any kind of warranty?

A Request

The lawman let me down
last night. He did not
listen to my request for a cinder
block sanctuary,
only one in the group sober
enough to tell him
my wife will kill me,
please lock me up tonight instead.
That left five rough miles
from the outskirts
to the bed skirts,
though I only made it to the stoop.

Under the stars, my head its own cold boulder
filled not with regret,
but the bastard heavy feeling that's fond
of sitting beside and tugging
at any ear that will beg a listen.

I should have reminded that lawman
that wheelmen made these
country roads, not autos.
We made them with our
deep tire grooves,
forming with repetition
a way to cross from one rural place
to one godforsaken other, simply
by refusing to give it a stop.
Relentless. Stubborn. Foolish,
as the wife would say. Or
any other name worth answering to.

Pickwick Tavern

This bar only takes cash
and didn't kick out the old man who fell asleep
in the corner on your birthday.

Remember that?
All the water rings on the table we
ran our hands through, touching
our fingers to our foreheads
to cool us down.

This bar has been here since the Depression,
so I suppose it's earned the right to say
who can slump, who can stay, how we pay.

And I think it's always been a dive bar
unlike its neighbors: the tire shop that's now
an art gallery; the pastry shop turned used
book store. There's even a theatre
set back from the crumbling red brick
road where people now gather
every Sunday to worship.

But you want to know what I think?
I think the need for a cold beer in a
sweaty pint glass in early August is so
universal, no one will try to turn this tavern
into anything else. No one should complain
that their credit cards are no good here.
No one should complain about the heat
or the overabundance of lawn mower beers.

No one will suggest this building be anything
else to keep up with the trends of urban change.

And no one will ask me to leave:
this old man
who misses you,
who never fails to finish his glass,
looking down for all the water rings we've made
laying my head down among them
at last to sleep.

Gruene, TX

I once drank a beer in the oldest dance hall in Texas
and years later, read a woman's anonymous online review:
Since 1878, the floorboards have been absorbing the voices
of every legendary country singer who's ever
stood on that stage. A palpable history.
Probably, I thought. Wood that old.

But still: what a bold thing to say.
Had she dropped her palms to the floor, reached out
the tips of her fingers to listen for that music?
Maybe the heel of her boot got stuck in a sticky liquor spill
and she'd said to herself, *this place reverberates.*

Maybe she knew a thing or two about floors, though.
I started to think of her as a girl who'd lingered for hours
in a windowless room of like-planks. That she'd often
slipped her small feet in chic satin shoes and danced
and danced, listening to the notes streaming up from the wood,
the music of every hour of practice, every flawless recital
living in that wood, waiting in those planks, living on through her
while she would dance and think of how we are all a little bound
to soak in the melodies and the voices and the footprints
of everyone who's ever danced before us.

By the end of July

The bricks in the road
carry their heat into the night.
I can walk there with no shoes,
the letter I wrote last spring
creased in my back pocket.

I know better than to venture a swim
in May. Instead, give Lake Michigan
a few weeks of this heat, and the fresh
water is a full tea kettle
cooling on the stove.

But I don't know why I
wrote that letter,
except to say
giving ink to words
makes me feel like I have accomplished
something. I have created a finished product
from a mess of raw materials, as if
some functional assembly line lives
inside me, and if everybody on it could just
move these idle feelings tidily along, carry
them from my heart to wherever it is
they are supposed to go in a uniform and
measured way—well.
That would be great.

Where to, though.

Forward.
Carry these words forward.

The letter has wrinkles and a stain from lemonade
but no address, no addressee, no postage.

In the morning, I can throw it in a blue mailbox
the way romantic people cast love letters at the ocean
in glass bottles, and the salty waves hold them in their fingertips
for a very long time before finally deciding
what exactly to do with them.

When I was small

I didn't understand
why my father drove
the car in silence.

Friends' parents played the radio
singing, thumping
their fingers along the steering wheel.

Then I had children of my own
and grew tired
joints and wider hips, and the ability to stare
out the window
in silence when Peace
stopped in for a quick visit
with her
lovely wife Silence.

Now I can drive for hours
with nothing on at all.

Now I can admire
the fine brickwork
of the fireplace,
the neat trim
of the window.

Ignore the long green
grass of the lawn
asking for a mow.
Ignore the dirty windowpanes.
Ignore it all for now.
Sit with the gentle way
my son balls his fists

bringing them to his eyes
telling me once again
it's time to dream
for awhile.

Finding a rifle under the bed

I.

On some beaches, the sand lays
clean and tan and warm, a veritable carpet
for those relentless waves.

But water chops away at whatever
land answers the call to border it.

There is not always a smooth
line between land and water.

II.

You stand a few feet back from the
shoreline with your gun

and I stand a few feet back from you,
the loud pop of the trigger,
the white clouds from your cigarette.

when it hits me

III.

you will always be a faceless mystery,
water and earth and smoke to me.

Property Line

The year my father died, the willow in the side yard followed suit. Which was weird because it had never fully decided to whom it belonged. Its roots were on my neighbor's property, but it shed its branches in our yard like it wanted me to provide hospice services when my own father was too far away for my daily care.

And we were overwhelmed already with the new baby. I wasn't up for the silent battle of wills with my reticent old neighbor, who did not smile at me and did not wave at me, but rather regarded me with a wary eye, choosing only once in a while to stand by the curtainless window so we could get a good look at each other.

"Do you think this is because I breastfeed in the sunroom?" I asked my husband. "And doesn't he know my father is dying?" We were in the lawn assembling a pile of sticks. The baby nestled close to my chest in his carrier. My husband shook his head and took from me the thick gnarled branch I hadn't realized I'd been squeezing.

By August, the war of the branches had hit a fever pitch. As they rained down, the telephone rang more frequently and the news got worse, and I paced the backyard, gathering branches from the weeping willow and glaring out the pale window wondering if a tree had ever been so aptly named. Maybe an Evergreen, I thought. But this felt personal.

Tall yard waste bags lined our house the morning I packed the baby's bag, then one for me. I had wept all night, shedding my grief as steadily as the tree. Was this the plan all along, then? To live 80 years in one place, grow tall while a parade of people lived by you, and then at the end of your life, some stranger cares for you while you die?

"It's time to go," my husband said. I had been staring at the hollow willow in the early dawn light when movement in the side window next door caught my eye. There he was. The old man was waving. I shifted my baby's weight to my left hip, held him close to my chin, raised my own hand like the arm of a strong tree, and waved back.

Woman in House

When I dream of my mother,
it is my bad conscience
surfacing.

That's what my dream dictionary
tells me.

She spoke to me
in my dream last night,
but you know
as well as I
how impossible it is to understand
what
mothers
and
figures
and lovers
and anyone else is trying to
say to us in our dreams.

It is as though their messages are spoken
backward or upside down,
from an ancient age.

Do you know what she
was trying to tell me?

Whatever it was,
she smiled
and laughed and
her laughter woke me,
uncovered me,
made me thumb once again through
that big book of symbols
looking for her on
any page I can.

The Real Bear

The real bear will be
hiding in June
when the radio plays a chorus
with notes and words so
generous and distinctive
I think yes,
that's him all right,
up there high in the tree.

The notes rain down like
shards of broken bark
on the forest floor.

What wilderness there is
inside of us.
What a thing to try to forget
or at least hide
in my mind's plane of memory.

I bet he climbed that tree
just because he could.

The chorus echoes the summer air
and I think yes,
the real bear will be
descending soon. There's no way
he'll go
for the honey.
He'll make his racket
all the way down, tear his
claws into the tree,
take a look at each of the oak's
wooden rings, counting them
one by one
til next year.

The News of the World

The news of the world will all be bad this morning,
so let's not listen. Let's press our hands instead on
cool lined paper, sink back into lavender sheets. A
deep sigh will do, too, and you drift back to sleep
with all your worries tucking themselves back
into the wrinkles around your brown eyes.

It's an odd life—well, perfectly ordinary—but strange
to craft a raft of our own without knowing how long
we'll all float here together, happy—Happy, though
the rest of the world seems to be a sea of discontent.
Content, though of course it is the way of the sea
to call us each away in turn to depths beyond our reach.

Once, I read an author write that death is someone
you love only living in the next room of the house.
They have not left; they are still there. Maybe you
catch footsteps from time to time, hear the sound
of their laughter over the coffee grinder, the crash
of water splattering in the kitchen sink.

But that is news for another morning, and these are words
of worry for another time, meant for me to read back
later. Later, like waves hitting the shore. Today when
you wake, we'll warm you with our bodies in turn,
guide you from dreams to daylight, and when you open
your hands for that first cup of coffee it will bring you

to life.

Colleen Alles is a native Michigander living in Grand Rapids. She completed a BA in English with an Option in Creative Writing from Michigan State University, and earned her master's from Wayne State University. Her fiction and poetry have appeared in literary magazines and other publications, including *Red Cedar Review, Peninsula Poets, Open Palm Print, Cardinal Sins, Write Michigan 2016 Anthology,* and others. Her first book of poetry, *Induction: Poems for my new Daughter* was published by Finishing Line Press (Georgetown, KY) in March, 2018. She works for a public library in West Michigan. When not writing, Colleen enjoys spending time with family, running, traveling, good coffee, and craft beer.

CPSIA information can be obtained
at www.ICGtesting.com
Printed in the USA
JSHW010619150919
1409JS00002B/32

9 781646 620197